Presented To
Cedar Mill Community Library

Purchased with a grant
from a 2009 family foundation

SUPER
CARS

BY **DENNY VON FINN**

BELLWETHER MEDIA • MINNEAPOLIS, MN

™

Are you ready to take it to the extreme?
Torque books thrust you into the action-packed world
of sports, vehicles, and adventure. These books may
include dirt, smoke, fire, and dangerous stunts.
WARNING: read at your own risk.

This edition first published in 2010 by Bellwether Media, Inc.

No part of this publication may be reproduced in whole or in part without written permission of the publisher. For information regarding permission, write to Bellwether Media, Inc., Attention: Permissions Department, 5357 Penn Avenue South, Minneapolis, MN, 55419.

Library of Congress Cataloging-in-Publication Data

Von Finn, Denny.
  Super cars / by Denny Von Finn.
     p. cm. – (Torque. The world's fastest)
  Includes bibliographical references and index.
  Summary: "Amazing photography accompanies engaging information about super cars. The combination of high-interest subject matter and light text is intended for students in grades 3 through 7" –Provided by publisher.
  ISBN 978-1-60014-289-5 (hardcover : alk. paper)
  1. Muscle cars--Juvenile literature. 2. Sports cars--Juvenile literature. I. Title.
  TL236.V676 2010
  629.222'1--dc22
                              2009013256

Printed in the United States of America.

CONTENTS

What Are Super Cars?

Super cars are the world's fastest **street-legal** automobiles. They provide a fast, exciting driving experience. All super cars can reach very high speeds. They also offer the driver great **handling**. Super cars are famous for their sleek and unusual designs.

A super car is a kind of sports car. Sports cars are quick, two-seat automobiles. They became popular after World War II. Automakers in the 1960s began building very powerful sports cars. They offered car **enthusiasts** the same excitement as auto racing. People called these extreme sports cars super cars.

Super cars are very expensive machines. Most of them cost more than $200,000. Expensive materials are needed for the high performance of a super car. Skilled **craftsmen** build super cars. They build them by hand. Each super car takes a long time to build. This long process makes each super car even more expensive.

Fast Fact

The most expensive super cars sell for nearly $2 million.

Super Car Technology

Most super car engines have at least eight **cylinders**. Some super cars have twelve cylinders. Cylinders provide plenty of room for the engine to burn fuel. This gives the super car its power and helps it reach incredible speeds. Many super cars can go more than 200 miles (322 kilometers) per hour!

Most super car engines are located behind the **cockpit**. The engine's weight pushes down on the rear wheels of the car. This increases the car's **traction**.

Great care is taken to **tune** a super car's **suspension system**. Good suspension and traction make a super car easy to handle. Good handling makes the super car fun to drive.

The outside of a super car is designed to help it go fast. The hood of a super car slants sharply to the road surface. The **chassis** is close to the ground. The driver and passenger must stoop to get inside. These **styling** features help the super car cut through the air more easily.

The Future of Super Cars

Super cars are defined by **acceleration**. An automobile must accelerate from 0 to 60 miles (96 kilometers) per hour in 4 seconds or less to be called a super car. Some super cars can do it in less than 3 seconds.

Future super cars may use **alternative fuels**. Such cars are still in the early stages of development. Alternative fuels are becoming popular because they pollute less than gasoline.

One alternative fuel is electricity. The Tesla Roadster is an electric car first manufactured in 2008. The Tesla Roadster offers the same speed, handling, and styling of many super cars.

Fast Fact

The 2009 Tesla Roadster can go from 0 to 60 miles (97 kilometers) per hour in under 4 seconds.

In 2005, a Bugatti Veyron became the fastest super car in the world. It reached 253 miles (407 kilometers) per hour!

People will always seek high speeds with super cars. The Bugatti Veyron is one of the fastest super cars ever built. Its 16-cylinder gasoline engine produces more than 1,001 **horsepower**. It can go from 0 to 62 miles (100 kilometers) per hour in just 2.5 seconds!

GLOSSARY

acceleration—how quickly a car gains speed

alternative fuels—sources of power other than gasoline

chassis—the frame of a car

cockpit—the area of a car where the driver and passenger sit

craftsmen—people who use great skill and care to create top-quality objects

cylinders—hollow chambers inside an engine where fuel is burned to create power

enthusiasts—people who enjoy a hobby, such as collecting and driving cars

handling—how easily a car steers

horsepower—a unit for measuring the power of an engine

street-legal—a vehicle that is considered safe for streets and highways

styling—the design and appearance of a car

suspension system—the springs and shock absorbers that connect the body of a vehicle to its wheels; the suspension system allows for a smooth ride.

traction—how well a car's tires grip the road surface

tune—to adjust for top performance

TO LEARN MORE

AT THE LIBRARY

Graham, Ian. *Sports Cars*. Chicago, Ill.: Heinemann, 2008.

Von Finn, Denny. *Sports Cars*. Minneapolis, Minn.: Bellwether Media, 2010.

Woods, Bob. *Hottest Sports Cars*. Berkeley Heights, N.J.: Enslow, 2007.

ON THE WEB

Learning more about super cars is as easy as 1, 2, 3.

1. Go to www.factsurfer.com.

2. Enter "super cars" into the search box.

3. Click the "Surf" button and you will see a list of related Web sites.

With factsurfer.com, finding more information is just a click away.

INDEX

The images in this book are reproduced through the courtesy of: oksana.perkins,
front cover, p. 13; Ron Kimball / Kimballstock, pp. 4-5, 10-11, 12, 16-17, 18-19;
culture-images GmbH / Alamy, pp. 6-7, 20-21; Maksim Toome, pp. 8-9; eikon / Age
Fotostock, p. 9 (upper); © Transtock Inc. / Alamy, pp. 14-15